KN✝CK

PRAYER BOOK

First published in 2018 by

 **columba**BOOKS

23 Merrion Square North,
Dublin 2, Co. Dublin
www.columbabooks.com

ISBN: 978-1-78218-298-6

Set in Freigh Text Pro 11/15
Cover and book design by Alba Esteban | Columba Books

All photographs Michael McLaughlin, except pages 10-11 and page 108
by Eamonn McCarthy (Image of Mayo) and page 46 by Maria Hunt, page
116 by James Wims and page 150 courtesy of Knock Shrine collection.
Illustrations pages 27-40 design by Jagoda (Shutterstock)

Printed by Jellyfish Solutions

KN⚲CK

PRAYER BOOK

Fr Richard Gibbons

columba
BOOKS

CONTENTS

PRAYERS TO OUR LADY

PRAYERS FOR FAMILY AND COMMUNITY LIFE

WORK PRAYERS

PRAYERS FOR MINISTRY

HEALING PRAYERS

SAINTS' PRAYERS

PRAYERS TO SAINTS

PRAYERS FOR CREATION

INTRODUCTION

"More things are wrought by prayer
than this world dreams of."
– Alfred Lord Tennyson

Tennyson's line here (a fuller verse of his is found within the book) is the inspiration for this short book of prayers.

The prayers within come from life lived in Knock and what Knock means to all the pilgrims, visitors, volunteers and parishioners that make up its story.

I myself find prayer difficult; I sometimes find the time to pray almost outside my grasp. I try to keep before me Pope St John Paul II's advice – "In doing the work of the Lord, do not forget the Lord of the work." I use various different techniques from the Divine Office, (prayer of the Church), to *Lectio Divina* (meditative prayer on Scripture), to favourite prayers I have brought with me throughout my life. It's not easy – let's just say from my early days in seminary, I knew I was not cut out for monastic life!

This prayer book then is a resource of different prayers and meditations for various different needs and times – some of them are familiar, some newly composed and some from other authors. They reflect the way we work in, live in and visit Knock. They range from our Novena prayers to Our Lady of Knock to prayers for workers, hospitality, healing, nature and dogs! Essentially this book is for those of you who may not get the chance to pray, have forgotten how to or would just like something simple and accessible to help you along the pilgrim road of life.

The best advice I can give you – and which the Lord gave to us (Matthew 6:6) – if you are starting again, is to simply find a quiet space, a room, chapel or outdoor area and be still. Bring to mind who or what you are praying for, offer the prayer and maybe focus for a while on a word or a line that strikes you (let God help!). Conclude with a prayer of thanksgiving for something good in your life (always be positive!). Then, finish with a Glory be to the Father... etc. and then the following:

Our Lady of Knock,
>   *pray for us.*

St Joseph,
>   *pray for us.*

St John the Evangelist,
>   *pray for us.*

Lamb of God, you take away the sins of the world,
>   *have mercy on us.*

Amen.

Well done! You've started again!

DAILY PRAYERS

POWER OF PRAYER

....

More things are wrought by prayer than this world
   dreams of.
Wherefore, let thy voice rise like a fountain for me
   night and day.
For what are men better than sheep or goats
that nourish a blind life within the brain,
if, knowing God, they lift not hands of prayer
both for themselves and those who call them
   friends?
For so the whole round Earth is every way bound
   by gold chains about the feet of God.
Amen.

....

Alfred, Lord Tennyson. From *Morte D'Arthur*

THE LORD'S PRAYER – OUR FATHER

Our Father, who art in Heaven,
hallowed be thy Name,
thy Kingdom come,
thy will be done,
on Earth as it is in Heaven.
Give us this day our daily bread.
And forgive us our trespasses,
as we forgive those
who trespass against us.
And lead us not into temptation,
but deliver us from evil.
Amen.

AN PHAIDIR

An Phaidir
Ár nAthair atá neamh,
go naofar d'anim,
Go dtaga do ríocht,
Go ndéantar do thoil ar an talamh
mar a dhéantar ar neamh.
Ár n-arán laethúil tabhair dúinn inniu,
agus maith dúinn ár bhfiacha,
mar a mhaithimidne ár bhféichiúna féin,
Agus ná lig sinn i gcathú,
ach saor sinn ó olc.
Áiméan.

HAIL MARY

Hail Mary, full of grace,
The Lord is with thee,
Blessed art thou among women,
and blessed is the fruit of thy womb, Jesus.
Holy May, Mother of God,
pray for us sinners,
now and at the hour of our death.
Amen.

'S É DO BHEATHA, A MHUIRE

'S é do bheatha, a Mhuire,
atá lán de ghrásta, tá an Tiarna leat.
Is beannaithe thú idir mhná,
agus is beannaithe toradh do bhroinne, Íosa.
A Naomh-Mhuire, a mháthair Dé,
guigh orainne na peacaigh,
anois agus ar uair ár mbáis.
Áiméan.

GLORY BE

Glory be to the Father,
and to the Son,
and to the Holy Spirit,
as it was in the beginning,
is now and ever shall be
world without end.
Amen.

GLÓIR DON ATHAIR

Glóir don Athair,
agus don Mhac,
agus don Spiorad Naomh.
Mar a bhí ar thús,
mar atá anois.
mar a bheas go brách,
le saol na saol.
Áiméan.

PRAYER FOR LIFE

Lord, your gift of life is precious to us.
Help us to appreciate and defend it
from conception to natural death
in a way that respects each other's human dignity
as well as giving glory to your will for us
as we journey together on Earth.
Amen.

Fr Richard Gibbons

PRAYER FOR THE DEAD

Eternal rest, grant unto them O Lord
and let perpetual light shine upon them.
May their souls and the souls of all the faithful
    departed,
through the mercy of God, rest in peace.
Amen.

COME HOLY SPIRIT

Come, Holy Spirit, fill the hearts of your faithful
and enkindle in them the fire of your love.

V. *Send forth your Spirit and they shall be created.*
R. *And you shalt renew the face of the earth.*

O God, who by the light of the Holy Spirit,
did instruct the hearts of the faithful,
grant that by the same Holy Spirit we may be truly
wise
and ever enjoy His consolations,
Through Christ Our Lord,
Amen.

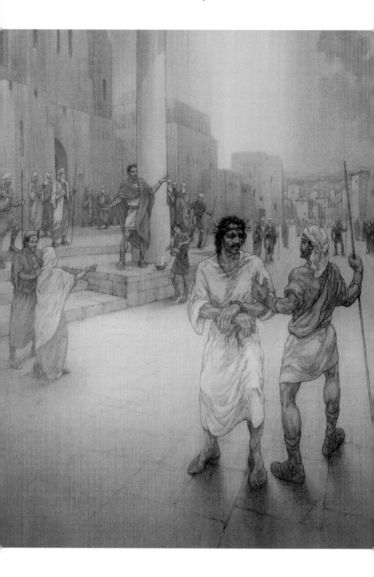

THE STATIONS OF THE CROSS

. . . .

I

Jesus is condemned to Death

V. *(Genuflecting) We adore you, O Christ, and praise you.*

R. *Because by your holy cross you have redeemed the world.*

Jesus, it was not Pilate alone, but my sins and the sins of all that condemned you to die. I am sorry for the contribution that my sins have made to your sufferings and death.

Glory be to the Father, and to the Son,
and to the Holy Spirit.
As it was in the beginning, is now, and
ever shall be, world without end. Amen.

II

Jesus takes up his cross

V. *(Genuflecting) We adore you, O Christ, and praise you.*

R. *Because by your holy cross you have redeemed the world.*

Jesus help me take up my cross and follow you. That cross may be for me ill-health, financial difficulties or having to suffer from the defects of others. Help me to accept my cross and carry it with you so that my feet may be then surely set on the road to salvation.

Glory be to the Father, and to the Son,
and to the Holy Spirit.
As it was in the beginning, is now, and
ever shall be, world without end. Amen.

III

Jesus falls the first time

V. *(Genuflecting) We adore you, O Christ, and praise you.*

R. *Because by your holy cross you have redeemed the world.*

Jesus, it was not the weight of the cross alone but of my sins which caused you to fall. Help me never to fall into serious sin but to watch and pray so that I may be delivered from the power of the evil one.

Glory be to the Father, and to the Son,
and to the Holy Spirit.
As it was in the beginning, is now, and
ever shall be, world without end. Amen.

IV

Jesus meets his mother

V. *(Genuflecting) We adore you, O Christ, and praise you.*

R. *Because by your holy cross you have redeemed the world.*

Mary, my mother, it was prophesied that Jesus was to be a sign that would be rejected. If I have ever rejected him in any way I now confess my sorrow. Grant me grace to repent of my sins, and to be truly reconciled to the love of your Son.

Glory be to the Father, and to the Son, and to the Holy Spirit. As it was in the beginning, is now, and ever shall be, world without end. Amen.

V

Simon of Cyrene helps Jesus to carry his cross

V. *(Genuflecting) We adore you, O Christ, and praise you.*

R. *Because by your holy cross you have redeemed the world.*

Jesus, your apostle Paul has said: "Bear one another's burdens, and so fulfil the law of Christ." (Gal. 6, 2) Grant that I may always try to bear with the faults of others. May I do all in my power to ease the burden of those who carry the cross after you. Let my sharing in their burdens be the fulfilling of your law.

Glory be to the Father, and to the Son,
and to the Holy Spirit.
As it was in the beginning, is now, and
ever shall be, world without end. Amen.

VI

Veronica wipes the face of Jesus

V. *(Genuflecting) We adore you, O Christ, and praise you.*

R. *Because by your holy cross you have redeemed the world.*

Jesus, help me to love and serve you in loving and serving the poor, the hungry, the sick and the distressed. Let me remember your words: "As you did it to one of the least of these my brethren, you did it to me". (Matt. 25, 40)

Glory be to the Father, and to the Son, and to the Holy Spirit.
As it was in the beginning, is now, and ever shall be, world without end. Amen.

VII

Jesus falls the second time

V. *(Genuflecting) We adore you, O Christ, and praise you.*

R. *Because by your holy cross you have redeemed the world.*

Jesus, if I should fall beneath the cross of suffering or of sorrow, give me the courage to rise again and to follow bravely after you.

Glory be to the Father, and to the Son, and to the Holy Spirit. As it was in the beginning, is now, and ever shall be, world without end. Amen.

VIII

The women of Jerusalem weep for our Lord

V. *(Genuflecting) We adore you, O Christ, and praise you.*

R. *Because by your holy cross you have redeemed the world.*

In your suffering, Jesus, you did not think of yourself, but of those who were to suffer on your behalf. Help me to rid myself of excessive self-love and self-pity.

Glory be to the Father, and to the Son,
and to the Holy Spirit.
As it was in the beginning, is now, and
ever shall be, world without end. Amen.

IX

Jesus falls the third time

V. *(Genuflecting) We adore you, O Christ, and praise you.*

R. *Because by your holy cross you have redeemed the world.*

Jesus, if I should ever fall into serious sin grant that I may not remain in that miserable state. May I, like you, rise to my feet and return to be reconciled to your loving forgiveness.

Glory be to the Father, and to the Son, and to the Holy Spirit.
As it was in the beginning, is now, and ever shall be, world without end. Amen.

X

Jesus is stripped of his clothes

V. *(Genuflecting) We adore you, O Christ, and praise you.*

R. *Because by your holy cross you have redeemed the world.*

Jesus, fill me with a spirit of true Christian shame and modesty. Grant that I, who am made in your image and likeness and whose body is the temple of your Holy Spirit, may always have respect and reverence for my own body and the bodies of others.

Glory be to the Father, and to the Son,
and to the Holy Spirit.
As it was in the beginning, is now, and
ever shall be, world without end. Amen.

XI

Jesus is nailed to the cross

V. *(Genuflecting) We adore you, O Christ, and praise you.*

R. *Because by your holy cross you have redeemed the world.*

Jesus, because you were like us in all things but sin, your body was sensitive to the slightest physical pain. When I have to suffer physical pain, help me to bear it by remembering your being nailed to the cross.

Glory be to the Father, and to the Son,
and to the Holy Spirit.
As it was in the beginning, is now, and
ever shall be, world without end. Amen.

XII

Jesus dies on the cross

V. *(Genuflecting) We adore you, O Christ, and praise you.*

R. *Because by your holy cross you have redeemed the world.*

Jesus, death has not been abolished in the world, but you by your death have transformed it. May your death be for me and for all, the gateway to eternal life. When my life on earth is ended, may I die in your love. Grant that you may receive my soul into your hands.

Glory be to the Father, and to the Son, and to the Holy Spirit.
As it was in the beginning, is now, and ever shall be, world without end. Amen.

XIII

Jesus is taken down from the cross

V. *(Genuflecting) We adore you, O Christ, and praise you.*

R. *Because by your holy cross you have redeemed the world.*

Mary, my Mother, you suffered with your Son in the work of our Redemption. May that Redemption bear fruit in our lives. May we, like the wheat grain that falls to the ground and dies, yield a harvest rich in works of faith and love.

Glory be to the Father, and to the Son,
and to the Holy Spirit.
As it was in the beginning, is now, and
ever shall be, world without end. Amen.

XIV
Jesus is placed in the tomb

V. *(Genuflecting) We adore you, O Christ, and praise you.*

R. *Because by your holy cross you have redeemed the world.*

Jesus, you suffered and died, but you rose again on the third day. You said: "I am the Resurrection and the Life." Grant that I, having shared in your suffering and death, may be worthy to share in the joy and the glory of your Resurrection. "Dying you destroyed our death, rising your restored our life".

Glory be to the Father, and to the Son,
and to the Holy Spirit.
As it was in the beginning, is now, and
ever shall be, world without end. Amen.

A MEDITATION

O Lord, support us all the day long,
until the shadows lengthen
and the evening comes,
and the busy world is hushed
and the fever of life is over
and our work is done.
Then in your mercy,
grant us a safe lodging and a holy rest,
and peace at last.
Amen.

Blessed John Henry Cardinal Newman

PRAYER BEFORE THE BLESSED SACRAMENT

O Sacrament most Holy,
O Sacrament Divine,
All praise and all thanksgiving,
Be every moment Thine.
Amen.

ANIMA CHRISTI

Soul of Christ, sanctify me
Body of Christ, save me
Blood of Christ, inebriate me
Water from Christ's side, wash me
Passion of Christ, strengthen me
O good Jesus, hear me
Within Thy wounds hide me
Suffer me not to be separated from Thee
From the malicious enemy defend me
In the hour of my death call me
And bid me come unto Thee
That I may praise Thee with Thy saints
and with Thy angels
Forever and ever
Amen.

THE DIVINE PRAISES

Blessed be God.

Blessed be His Holy Name.

Blessed be Jesus Christ, true God and true Man.

Blessed be the Name of Jesus.

Blessed be His Most Sacred Heart.

Blessed be His Most Precious Blood.

Blessed be Jesus in the Most Holy Sacrament of the Altar.

Blessed be the Holy Spirit, the Paraclete.

Blessed be the great Mother of God, Mary most Holy.

Blessed be her Holy and Immaculate Conception.

Blessed be her Glorious Assumption.

Blessed be the Name of Mary, Virgin and Mother.

Blessed be St Joseph, her most chaste spouse.

Blessed be God in His Angels and in His Saints.

Amen.

THE APOSTLES' CREED

I believe in God,
the Father Almighty
Creator of Heaven and Earth.
And in Jesus Christ,
His only Son, Our Lord
Who was conceived by the Holy Spirit,
born of the Virgin Mary,
suffered under Pontius Pilate,
was crucified, died and was buried;
He descended into Hell;
on the third day He rose again from the dead;
He ascended into Heaven,
and is seated at the right hand
of God the Father Almighty;
from there He will come to judge
the living and the dead.
I believe in the Holy Spirit,
the holy Catholic Church,
the communion of saints,
the forgiveness of sins,
the resurrection of the body,
and life everlasting.
Amen.

THE CHAPLET OF THE DIVINE MERCY

The Chaplet of Mercy is recited using ordinary rosary beads of five decades.

1. MAKE THE SIGN OF THE CROSS

In the name of the Father, and of the Son, and of the Holy Spirit. Amen.

2. OPTIONAL OPENING PRAYERS

You expired, Jesus, but the source of life gushed forth for souls, and the ocean of mercy opened up for the whole world. O Fount of Life, unfathomable Divine Mercy, envelop the whole world and empty Yourself out upon us.

(Repeat three times)

O Blood and Water, which gushed forth from the Heart of Jesus as a fountain of Mercy for us, I trust in You!

3. OUR FATHER

Our Father, Who art in heaven, hallowed be Thy name; Thy kingdom come; Thy will be done on earth as it is in heaven. Give us this day our daily bread; and forgive us our trespasses as we forgive those who trespass against us; and lead us not into temptation, but deliver us from evil. Amen.

4. HAIL MARY

Hail Mary, full of grace. The Lord is with thee. Blessed art thou amongst women, and blessed is the fruit of thy womb, Jesus.

Holy Mary, Mother of God, pray for us sinners, now and at the hour of our death. Amen.

5. THE APOSTLE'S CREED

I believe in God, the Father almighty, Creator of heaven and earth, and in Jesus Christ, His only Son, our Lord, who was conceived by the Holy Spirit, born of the Virgin Mary, suffered under Pontius Pilate, was crucified, died and was buried; He descended into hell; on the third day He rose again from the dead; He ascended into heaven, and is seated at the right hand of God the Father almighty; from there He will come to judge the living and the dead.

I believe in the Holy Spirit, the holy Catholic Church, the communion of saints, the forgiveness of sins, the resurrection of the body, and life everlasting. Amen.

6. THE ETERNAL FATHER

Eternal Father, I offer you the Body and Blood, Soul and Divinity of Your Dearly Beloved Son, Our Lord, Jesus Christ, in atonement for our sins and those of the whole world.

7. ON THE TEN SMALL BEADS OF EACH DECADE

For the sake of His sorrowful Passion, have mercy on us and on the whole world.

8. REPEAT FOR THE REMAINING DECADES

Saying the "Eternal Father" (6) on the "Our Father" bead and then 10 "For the sake of His sorrowful Passion" (7) on the following "Hail Mary" beads.

9. CONCLUDE WITH HOLY GOD (*Repeat three times*)

Holy God, Holy Mighty One, Holy Immortal One, have mercy on us and on the whole world.

10. OPTIONAL CLOSING PRAYER

Eternal God, in whom mercy is endless and the treasury of compassion — inexhaustible, look kindly upon us and increase Your mercy in us, that in difficult moments we might not despair nor become despondent, but with great confidence submit ourselves to Your holy will, which is Love and Mercy itself.

PRAYERS FOR THE HOLY SOULS

Lord, Archdeacon Cavanagh offered one hundred Masses for the Holy Souls before the Apparition of 1879, look with love upon all souls in Purgatory and hear the prayers of your people on Earth and the Saints in Heaven which are offered for them.

May you embrace them in the joys of everlasting life. Amen.

Fr Richard Gibbons

Eternal Father, I offer you the most precious blood of thy Divine Son, Jesus, in union with the Masses said throughout the world today for all the Holy Souls in Purgatory, for sinners everywhere, for sinners in the Universal Church, for those in my own home and in my family.

Amen.

St Gertrude, 13th Century

PRAYER FOR TODAY

Lord, today I choose to release
all that holds me back.
Help me to let go of the past,
to let go of bitterness, to let go
of failures and missed opportunities.
Help me today to embrace your
grace in my life, that I may live it
to the full and help me be a blessing
to others.
Amen.

Fr Richard Gibbons

GRACE BEFORE MEALS

As we work towards the day
when the poor are no longer hungry;
when all food producers are treated fairly;
when the fortunate are no longer greedy;
when the Earth is treated with respect;
Lord God, we are grateful for all you have
    provided,
we give thanks for what we are about to share.
Amen.

GRACE AFTER MEALS

Lord we are grateful to You
for the food we have eaten,
the company we have enjoyed
and the gift of sharing what we have to offer.
Amen.

Fr Richard Gibbons

GUARDIAN ANGEL PRAYER

Angel of God, my guardian dear
to whom His love commits me here,
ever this day (night) be at my side
to light and guard, to rule and guide.
Amen.

CHILDREN'S BEDTIME PRAYER

Now I lay me down to sleep
I pray the Lord my soul to keep.
If I die before I wake,
I pray the Lord my soul to take.
See me safely through the night
and wake me with the morning light.
Amen.

PRAYER AT THE END OF THE DAY

This prayer might be recited at the end of the evening meal, when the members of the family are still together. The six parts might be said by different members, all joining in the responses. The prayer could conclude with the Rosary, or a part of it.

1. At the end of the day we praise you, Lord.
    We thank you for all the graces that have come
      to us from your hands.
    For bringing us safely through this day
    V. *We thank you, Lord*
    R. *From our hearts we thank you.*

    For the work you have given us to do
    V. *We thank you, Lord*
    R. *From our hearts we thank you.*

    For the food you have given us to eat
    V. *We thank you, Lord*
    R. *From our hearts we thank you.*

    For all we have learned and received from others
    V. *We thank you, Lord*
    R. *From our hearts we thank you.*

2. Forgive us the faults we have committed this day.
    For our laziness, our neglect of others, our
    want of love.
    V. We ask your mercy, Lord.
    R. For we are truly sorry.

3. Pour down your blessings on our family.
    May we all be one, as you are one.
    In generosity and love.
    We forgive and ask forgiveness this night
    For any sharp word we spoke today
    Or anything we did in anger or in haste.
    V. Lord, hear us
    R. And answer our prayer.

4. We remember those who have died...
    V. Grant them rest
    R. Lord, grant them eternal rest.

5. We pray for the whole world
    The sick, the lonely, and all who suffer injustice;
    Lord, help us to help them.
    Bless the people of our parish.
    Keep its priests, teachers, parents and children
    Always in your love.

    (other particular intentions may be added here)

V. *Lord, hear us*
R. *And answer our prayer.*

6. Visit, O Lord, this house.
    Keep it safe from all harm and danger.
    Protect our property.
    May your holy angels keep us in peace
    And may your blessings be always upon us,
    Through Jesus Christ, your Son, our Lord,
    Who lives and reigns with you
    In the unity of the Holy Spirit,
    One God for ever and ever. Amen.

Tuam Liturgical Commision

NIGHT PRAYER

At last all powerful Master
You give leave to your servant
to go in peace, according to your promise.
For my eyes have seen your salvation
which you have prepared for all nations
the light to enlighten the Gentiles
and give glory to Israel your people.
Nunc Dimittis
Amen.

Nunc Dimittis, Luke 2: 29-32

Prayers to
Our Lady

NOVENA TO OUR LADY OF KNOCK

....

14th to 22nd August

In the name of the Father, and of the Son,
and of the Holy Spirit. Amen.

Give praise to the Father Almighty,
To His Son, Jesus Christ the Lord,
To the Spirit who lives in our hearts,
Both now and forever. Amen.

*****

Our Lady of Knock, Queen of Ireland, you gave hope to your people in a time of distress, and comforted them in sorrow. You have inspired countless pilgrims to pray with confidence to your divine Son, remembering His promise, "Ask and you shall receive, seek and you shall find."

Help me to remember that we are all pilgrims on the road to Heaven. Fill me with love and concern for my brothers and sisters in Christ, especially those who live with me. Comfort me when I am sick, lonely or depressed. Teach me how to take part ever more reverently in the Holy Mass. Give me a greater love of Jesus in the Blessed Sacrament. Pray for me now and at the hour of my death. Amen.

Lamb of God, you take away the sins of the world;
Have mercy on us.
Lamb of God, you take away the sins of the world;
Have mercy on us.
Lamb of God, you take away the sins of the world;
Grant us peace.

*****

St Joseph,
Chosen by God to be
The Husband of Mary,
The Protector of the Holy Family,
The Guardian of the Church.
Protect all families
in their work and recreation
and guard us on our journey through life.

(Repeat – Lamb of God, you take away the sins of the world...)

St John,
Beloved Disciple of the Lord, Faithful Priest.
Teacher of the Word of God.
Help us to hunger for the Word.
To be loyal to the Mass
And to love one another

(Repeat – Lamb of God, you take away the sins of the world...)

Our Lady of Knock	*Pray for us*
Refuge of sinners	*Pray for us*
Queen Assumed into Heaven	*Pray for us*
Queen of the Rosary	*Pray for us*
Mother of Nazareth	*Pray for us*
Queen of Virgins	*Pray for us*
Help of Christians	*Pray for us*
Health of the Sick	*Pray for us*
Queen of Peace	*Pray for us*
Our Lady, Queen and Mother	*Pray for us*
Our Lady, Mother of the Church	*Pray for us*

(Here mention your own special intentions)

*****

With the angels and saints, let us pray:
Give praise to the Father Almighty,
To His Son, Jesus Christ the Lord,
To the Spirit who lives in our hearts,
Both now and forever.
Amen.

PILGRIM'S PRAYER FROM KNOCK SHRINE

Our Lady of Knock, Queen of Ireland,
Glorious in your Assumption and Coronation,
Be our strength, our hope, our consolation.

Our Lady of Knock, Mother of the Church!
Help and support us your pilgrim people,
As we journey through life.
Our Lady of Knock, Health of the Sick!
Obtain comfort and healing,
For all who confide in you.

Our Lady of Knock, Mystical Rose!
Take our petitions to Jesus Your Son,
Pray for us now and in every need.

Our Lady of Knock, Queen of Peace!
Obtain peace from our land,
And for all the nations of the earth.

Lamb of God,
You take away the sins of the world,
Grant us pardon and peace.
Lamb of God,
Perfect symbol for the Eucharist,
Teach us the significance of the Mass.

Lamb of God,
Our thanks to You, redeeming Lord,
For our ransom slain but now gloriously risen.

All you holy Angels of Knock,
Inspire us to imitate your adoration,
In the presence of the Eucharistic Lamb.

St Joseph, Spouse of Mary,
Guardian of the universal Church,
Protect us by your powerful intercession.

St John, Beloved Disciple of the Lord,
Help us to eagerly accept the Word of God,
And to love one another.
Amen.

....
Knock Shrine

THE ROSARY

....

Begin with the Apostles Creed, followed by Our Father, three Hail Marys and a Glory Be (For the Pope's intentions). If you wish, use the scripture references as meditations to accompany and focus your prayer.

JOYFUL MYSTERIES (MON & SAT)

1. The Annunciation (Lk 1:26-38)
2. The Visitation (Lk 1:39-45)
3. The Nativity (Lk 2:1-20)
4. The Presentation (Lk 2:22-40)
5. The Finding of Jesus in the Temple (Lk 2:41-52)

THE SORROWFUL MYSTERIES (TUES & FRI)

1. The Agony in the Garden (Mk 14:32-42)
2. The Scourging at the Pillar (Mt 27:26)
3. The Crowning with Thorns (Jn 19:2)
4. The Carrying of the Cross (Jn 19:16 -18)
5. The Crucifixion (Mt 27:32-56)

The Glorious Mysteries (Wed & Sun)

1. The Resurrection (Jn 19:40 – 20:18)
2. The Ascension (Lk 24:31)
3. The Descent of the Holy Spirit (Acts 2:1-13)
4. The Assumption (Rev 12:1)
5. The Coronation of the Blessed Virgin Mary (1 Cor 15:54)

The Mysteries of Light (Thurs)

1. The Baptism in the Jordan (Mt 3:13-17)
2. The Wedding of Cana (Jn 2:1-12)
3. The Proclamation of the Kingdom (Mk 1:14)
4. The Transfiguration (Lk 9:28-36)
5. The Institution of the Eucharist (Mk 14:22-24)

Hail Holy Queen

Hail, Holy Queen, Mother of Mercy, hail our life, our sweetness and our hope. To thee do we cry, poor banished children of Eve. To thee do we send up our sighs, mourning and weeping in this valley of tears. Turn then, most gracious advocate, thine eyes of Mercy towards us and after this our exile, show unto us the blessed fruit of thy womb, Jesus. O clement, O loving, O sweet Virgin Mary!

V. *Pray for us, O holy Mother of God.*

R. *That we may be made worthy of the promises of Christ.*

Let us pray:

O God,
whose only begotten Son, by His life, death and resurrection, has purchased for us the rewards of eternal salvation. Grant, we beseech thee, that while meditating on these mysteries of the most holy rosary of the Blessed Virgin Mary, that we may both imitate what they contain and obtain what they promise, through Christ our Lord.
Amen.

A PRAYER TO OUR BLESSED LADY FOR THOSE WHO ARE GROWING OLD

Take my hand, O Blessed Mother,
hold me firmly lest I fall.
I am nervous when I am walking
and to thee I humbly call.
Guide me over every crossing,
watch me when I'm on the stairs.
Let me know you are beside me,
listen to my fervent prayer.
Bring me to my destination
with you safely every day.
Help me with each undertaking
as the hours they pass away.
And when the evening falls upon me,
and I fear to be alone.
Take my hand O Blessed Mother,
please stay with me my home.
Amen.

TO CHRIST AND HIS MOTHER

O Christ Jesus, have mercy on us,
and O glorious Virgin, pray for us.
O Mother of God, Guiding Star,
O Queen of Paradise, comfort and help us
and obtain for us, from your Child,
the light of glory.
light of lights and vision of the Trinity
and the grace of patience in the face of injustice.
Amen.

DO CHÍOST AGUS DÁ MHÁTHAIR

A Íosa Críost, déan trócaire orainn
's a Mhaighdean ghlórmhar, guigh orainn.
A Mháthair Dé, a réalt an eolais,
a Bhanríon Pharthais, fortaigh is fóir orainn
agus faigh ó d'Leanbh dúinn solas na glóire,
radharc ar do theaghlach le d'mhórchomhachta
solas na soilse agus radharc na Tríonóide
agus grásta na foighne in aghaidh na héagóra.
Áiméan.

MEMORARE

....

Remember, O most gracious Virgin Mary
that never was it known
that anyone who fled to your protection,
implored your help or sought your intercession
was left unaided.
Inspired with this confidence, I fly unto you,
O Virgin of Virgins my Mother;
to you do I come before you I stand
sinful and sorrowful;
O Mother of the Word Incarnate
despise not my petitions but in your clemency
hear and answer me.
Amen.

....

St Bernard of Clairvaux

AN CUIMHNIGH

Cuimhnigh, a Mhaighdean Mhuire róghrámhar
nár chualathas trácht ar éinne
riamh a chuir é féin faoi do choimirce
ná a d'iarr cabhair ort ná a d'impigh
d'idirghuí is gur theip tú air.
Lán de mhuinín asat, dá bhrí sin,
rithimse chugat, a Mhaighdean na maighdean
is a Mháthair. Is chugatsa a thagaim,
is os do comhair a sheasaim, i mo
pheacach bocht atuirseach.
Ó a Mháthair an Aonmhic, ná diúltaigh
Do m'urnaithe ach éist leo go trócaireach
Agus freagair iad.
Áiméan.

OUR LADY OF GRACE

O Mary of Graces
and Mother of God
May I tread in the path
that the righteous have trod

May you save me
from evil's control
and may you save me in body and soul

May you save me
by land and by sea
And may you save me from tortures to be

May the guard of Angels
around me abide
And may God be before me and God at my side.
Amen.

A MHUIRE NA NGRÁS

A Mhuire na Grás,
A Mháthair Mhic Dé,
Go gcuire tú ar mo leas mé.

Go sábhála tú mé
Ar gach uile olc
Go sábhála tú mé idir anam is chorp

Go sábhála tú mé
Ar muir agus ar tír,
Go sábhála tú mé
Ar lic na bpain

Garda na n-aingeal
os mo choinn,
Dia romham agus Dia liom.
Áiméan.

HAIL HOLY QUEEN

Hail, holy Queen,
Mother of mercy,
hail, our life, our sweetness and our hope.
To thee do we cry, poor banished children of Eve.
To thee do we send up our sighs, mourning and
    weeping
In this vale of tears.
Turn, then, most gracious advocate,
thine eyes of mercy toward us,
and after this, our exile,
show unto us the blessed fruit of thy womb, Jesus.
O clement, O loving, O sweet
Virgin Mary.
Amen.

SALVE REGINA

Salve Regina
Mater misericordiae
Vita, dulcedo, et spes nostra, salve.
Ad te clamamus exsules filii Hevae.
Ad te suspiramus, gementes et flentes
In hac lacrimarum valle.
Eia ergo, Advocata nostra,
Illos tuos misericordes oculos ad nos converte.
Et Iesum, benedictum fructum ventris tui,
Nobis post hoc exsilium ostende,
O clemens, O pia, O dulcis
Virgo Maria.
Amen.

THE ANGELUS

....

V. *The angel of the Lord declared unto Mary.*

R. *and she conceived of the Holy Spirit.*

Hail Mary, full of grace,
The Lord is with thee,
Blessed art thou among women,
and blessed is the fruit of thy womb, Jesus.
Holy Mary, Mother of God,
pray for us sinners,
now and at the hour of our death.
Amen.

V. *Behold the handmaid of the Lord.*

R. *Be it done onto me according to thy word.*

(Repeat – Hail Mery)

V. *And the Word was made flesh.*

R. *And dwelt among us.*

(Repeat – Hail Mery)

V. *Pray for us O holy Mother of God.*

R. *That we may be made worthy of the promises of Christ.*

Let us pray:

Pour forth we beseech thee, O Lord, thy grace
unto our hearts that we to whom the
incarnation of Christ was made known by
the message of an angel, may by his passion
and cross be brought to the glory of
His resurrection. Through the same Jesus Christ
Our Lord.
Amen.

REGINA CAELI

The Regina Caeli is sung or recited in place of the Angelus during the Easter Season, from Holy Saturday to Pentecost Sunday.

*****

Regína caeli, laetáre. Allelúia:
Quia quem meruisti portare. Allelúia,
Resurréxit, sicut dixit. Allelúia,
Ora pro nobis, Deum. Allelúia.
Gaude et lætáre, Virgo María. Allelúia.
Quia surréxit Dóminus vere. Allelúia.

Orémus:
Deus, qui per resurrectiónem Fílii tui, Dómini nostri Iesu Christi, mundum laetificáre dignátus es: praesta, quaésumus; ut, per eius Genitrícem Vírginem Maríam, perpétuae capiámus gáudia vitae. Per eúndem Christum Dóminum nostrum. Amen.

QUEEN OF HEAVEN

Queen of Heaven, rejoice! Alleluia:
For He whom you did merit to bear. Alleluia.
Has risen, as He said. Alleluia.
Pray for us to God. Alleluia.
Rejoice and be glad, O Virgin Mary. Alleluia.
For the Lord has truly risen. Alleluia.

Let us pray:
O God, who gave joy to the world through the resurrection of your Son, Our Lord Jesus Christ grant, we beseech you, that through the intercession of the Virgin Mary, his Mother, we may obtain the joys of everlasting life. Through the same Christ our Lord.
Amen.

FAMILY AND COMMUNITY PRAYERS

PRAYER TO THE HOLY FAMILY

Jesus, Mary and Joseph,
in you we contemplate
the splendour of true love;
to you we turn with trust.
Holy Family of Nazareth,
grant that our families too
may be places of communion and prayer,
authentic schools of Gospel
and small domestic churches.
Holy Family of Nazareth,
may families never again experience
violence, rejection and division;
may all who have been hurt or scandalised
find ready comfort and healing.
Holy Family of Nazareth,
make us once more mindful
of the sacredness and inviolability of the family,
and its beauty in God's plan.
Jesus, Mary and Joseph,
graciously hear our prayer.
Amen.

Pope Francis, *Amoris Laetitia*, 325

AN OLD CANDLE PRAYER

Lord,
May this candle
Be light for you,
To enlighten me
In my difficulties and decisions.
May it be a fire
For you to burn out,
All pride, selfishness and impurity.
May it be our flame
For you to bring warmth to my heart
Towards my family and my neighbours
And all those who meet me.
Through the prayers of Mary, virgin and mother,
I place in your care those I come to remember,
    especially... *(Name)*.
I cannot stay long here with you,
In leaving this candle,
I wish to give you everything of myself,
Help me to continue in prayer
all I do this day.
Amen.

PRAYER OF ABANDONMENT

Father,
I abandon myself into your hands;
do with me what you will.
Whatever you may do, I thank you:
I am ready for all, I accept all.
Let only your will be done in me,
and in all your creatures -
I wish no more than this, O Lord.
Into your hands I commend my soul:
I offer it to you with all the love of my heart,
for I love you, Lord, and so need to give myself,
to surrender myself into your hands without
    reserve,
and with boundless confidence, for you are my
    Father.
Amen.

Charles de Foucauld

FAMILY PRAYER

....

Father, bless our family and keep us safe in your
    loving care.
May Mary our mother give us the wisdom to see
    You in our joys and sorrows,
our triumphs and failures.
May Jesus Your Son help us to support one
    another and heal us of any wounds and hurt
    that become part of family life.
Keep us true to your Son Jesus in the practice of
    our faith and in our love for one another.
In the fullness of time O Lord,
unite us with our deceased family members in
    Your eternal home.
Amen.

....

Fr Richard Gibbons

PRAYER FOR PARENTS

Lord, thank you for my children;
I know they are a gift from you.
Daily I need your strength and wisdom
to lead them on the right path.
Give me patience and a joyful heart;
let me be an example of your love and forgiveness.
Thank you, Father, for the gift of being a parent.
Amen.

SERENITY PRAYER FOR PARENTS

(Just for some fun!)

God grant me the serenity to
accept the annoying things
that my kids do, that I cannot change.
The patience to endure the endless nagging
that I will have to do to change the things I can.
And just enough wine to know the difference!

PRAYER FOR GRANDPARENTS

Lord Jesus,
you were born of the Virgin Mary,
the daughter of Saints Joachim and Anne.
Look with love on grandparents the world over.
Protect them!
They are a source of enrichment for families, for
the Church and for all of society.
Support them!
As they grow older,
may they continue to be for their families
strong pillars of Gospel faith,
guardians of noble domestic ideals,
living treasuries of sound religious traditions.
Make them teachers of wisdom and courage, that
they may pass on to future generations the fruits of
their mature human and spiritual experience.

Lord Jesus,
help families and society to value
the presence and role of grandparents.
May they never be ignored or excluded,
but always encounter respect and love.
Help them to live serenely and to feel welcomed
in all the years of life which you give them.
Mary, Mother of all the living,

keep grandparents constantly in your care,
accompany them on their earthly pilgrimage,
and by our prayers, grant that all families
may one day be reunited in our heavenly homeland,
where you await all humanity
for the great embrace of life without end.
Amen.

Benedict XVI

PRAYER FOR YOUNG PEOPLE

Lord, we pray that you guide and protect
young people and all who work with them.
Be with them as they experience sorrow and joy,
success and failure, sickness and health.
Encourage them to make the right decisions
as they journey through life and help them to
know your presence in their lives as
you walk by their side.
Amen.

Fr Richard Gibbons

LEAVE YOUR MARK

Lord,
Help us to be
Free
Happy
Fulfilled
Hopeful for the future.

Help us to realise that together we can
Make a difference
Blaze new trails
Open up new horizons
Spread joy, hope, love and peace.

Help us to believe
That God expects something special from us
That He has great hopes and dreams for us
and for our world.

Guide us
In times of doubt
In times of darkness
In times of disappointment

Teach us
How to pray
How to trust in your steadfast friendship and care
for each one of us.

Bless
Our families
Our friends
All who walk with us along the journey of life.

May we be open
To experience a new Pentecost moment,
To take risks
To reach out
To build bridges
To nurture friendships
To leave our mark on life, on history and on our
common home.
Amen.

Sr Teresa Nolan and 'Friends in Faith' group,
Mercy Secondary School, Tuam, Co. Galway

PRAYER FOR EXPECTANT MOTHERS

O God, my Father,
may the little one
that lies close to my heart
grow strong and perfect
to serve that purpose
for which he or she
is to be born.

O Mary, Mother of all
mothers, guide and protect
me in pregnancy.

In childbirth,
may I be brave and confident
in your care and presence.

May I use with skill
and understanding
the great gift of motherhood
in the years that lie ahead.
Amen.

Family Life & Prayer Centre, Knock Shrine

PRAYER FOR THE TRAVELLER COMMUNITY

Lord God, you are the source of life and love for
    the whole human family.
You know each of us by name and you cherish us
    without distinction.
Teach us, Lord, to respect one another's
    differences
and help us by your Son's example to reach out to
    all in understanding and peace.
We ask you Lord to bless our country's Traveller
    community,
may they live free from prejudice and know your
    love in good times and bad.
May they be encouraged to build up their local
    community
and your Kingdom in trust and solidarity with
    their neighbours.
Amen.

Fr Richard Gibbons

WORK PRAYERS

PRAYER FOR EXAM TIME

Lord, be with me as I begin my exams,
help me to think clearly,
to be calm and to express my answers accurately.
Help me to realise that
you are with me throughout my life
and with your Spirit to guide me
I may reach my full potential.
Amen.

Fr Richard Gibbons

A TEACHER'S PRAYER

Lord,
may I be a teacher both knowledgeable and kind
Help me to encourage each young
and growing mind
May my faith be evident in all I say and do
As I share the many lessons
that I have learned from you.
Amen.

(Unknown)

THE GARDENER'S PRAYER

I have worked in the fertile earth
and planted a garden;
so I know what faith is.
I have listened to the birds
carolling in the morning and at dusk;
so I know what music is.
I have seen the morning
without clouds after showers;
so I know what beauty is.
I have seen the miracle of spring,
the fruition of summer
and the beauty of autumn,
followed by the repose of winter;
so I know what life is.
Because I have perceived
all of those things,
I know what God is.
Amen.

PRAYER FOR DOCTORS, NURSES AND MEDICAL STAFF

Lord, you have made us to give you glory in mind, body and spirit. Help me to care for and be compassionate to all my patients in times of illness. Guide me in improving my knowledge and skill so that I may bring comfort and healing to all who are entrusted to my care.

Through the intercession of St Luke and the example of the Good Samaritan, may I always bear witness to you in promoting the Gospel of life, from conception to natural end and respect the dignity of each person.

Amen.

Fr Richard Gibbons

PRAYER FOR ALL WHO WORK IN HOSPITALITY

Lord, you are a God who opens your heart to all.

You gave us your Son, Jesus, to show us the way home.

In the story of the Prodigal Son, you welcome us home through forgiveness;

In the wedding feast of Cana, you show us your generosity of spirit in time of need;

In the meals your Son had with his disciples, Zaccheus, Martha and Mary and others, you hold before us the importance of table fellowship and friendship;

In the Eucharist, you give us the food of everlasting life.

Lord, may all who work in hotels, homes, cafés, and all areas of hospitality be examples of welcome, humour and kindness to all who visit.

Grant us patience when needed, a welcoming smile and thankfulness for all who spend time with us.

May we be for others the reflection of your love for us.

Amen.

Fr Richard Gibbons

A PRAYER FOR ALL WHO WORK AT KNOCK AIRPORT

Lord, Your inspiration helped Msgr Horan to build this airport to bring your message of hope and love to the world and in turn, to bring the world to Knock where people experience your peace, healing and forgiveness.

You have also inspired this place to be a source of employment and economic development.

Help all of us who work in this special place not to forget this legacy and in our work to be joyful, dutiful and kind to all who pass through this airport.

Grant your protection to all who travel.

Amen.

Fr Richard Gibbons

ST JOSEPH THE WORKER

St Joseph, you worked to provide a loving and supportive home for Mary and Jesus. Help me in my work to be as dedicated as you. Help me to be creative and productive and to see the hand of God in all I do. When my work is rewarding teach me to be thankful, when it is unrewarding or tiring help me to persevere or seek another path which gives meaning to my life. If I am unemployed, guide me in seeking work that will give me dignity and go towards building up the Kingdom of God.
Amen.

Fr Richard Gibbons

PRAYER FOR ARTISTS AND MUSICIANS

O Lord of all creation who made
the world to be a source of beauty
and joy reflecting your presence, I thank
you for the skill and ability to create and compose.
Give me the inspiration and enlightenment to
continue to be your instrument in my work.
Amen.

Fr Richard Gibbons

PRAYERS FOR MINISTRY

PRAYER FOR ALL IN RELIGIOUS AND CONSECRATED LIFE

Heavenly Father, look with care and love on those who have dedicated their lives to you through the Religious and Consecrated life.

May their lives of selflessness in your service bring comfort to all who seek their prayers and wisdom.

May they be sustained in their charism and mission to bring your love into the hearts of all who wish to draw nearer to you.

May their outreach, contemplative or active in the local community, give witness to the power of prayer at work for the building up of your Kingdom.

In times of personal trials and in difficulty in living community life, may you Lord guide them in seeing once again the origin of their vocation in your service and the service of others.

At the end of this life, may they rejoice in the hospitality of our heavenly homeland.

Amen.

Fr Richard Gibbons

PRAYER FOR PARISH COUNCILS

Lord, be with us as we enter
into this time of prayer and planning
for the building up of your Kingdom
in this Parish of *(Name)*
Help us Lord, to see your wisdom
in the talents and abilities which lie within us.
May we listen and share,
may we appreciate the call to serve
which you offer us for the good of our parish.
And may we face all our challenges
knowing that without you in our lives
nothing is possible.
Amen.

Fr Richard Gibbons

PRAYER FOR VOLUNTEERS

Lord, as I give of my time and effort
to help where I am needed,
grant me the grace to understand
that I am building up your Kingdom.
Help me to be kind and generous hearted,
knowing that by good works I seek rewards
not in this life but in the next.
Amen.

Fr Richard Gibbons

PILGRIM'S PRAYER

As I journey on this path of life, help me Lord
to walk in the light of your word.
Keep me safe, give me hope
and answer my prayers.
Give me the heart of a pilgrim
to seek your will in my life.
And at the end of life's way,
lead me into the safety
of your eternal Kingdom.
Amen.

Fr Richard Gibbons

A PRAYER FOR VOCATIONS TO THE PRIESTHOOD

Lady of Knock,
Shepherdess of the Lamb of God,
from the altar of the cross
the Saviour entrusted us
to your motherly care.
Ask God to send priestly vocations
to the Diocese/Order *(Name)*
Shepherd those whom God
is calling to the priesthood.
May they answer God's call
with courage, generosity and wisdom.
Saint Joseph,
Shepherd of the Holy Family.
Intercede for all families of our Diocese/Order.
May parents help and encourage
each child
to follow the vocation
to which God is calling them.
Saint John,
Bishop and Shepherd.
You rested close to the heart of the Lord.
Intercede for the bishop and priests of *(Name)*
May strength come to them
from their closeness

to the heart of Christ,
and so may they shepherd
their people
in such a loving manner
as to inspire others
to answer the priestly calling.
Jesus,
Shepherd, Lamb, Sacrifice.
Give shepherds
similar to your heart
to the people of (*Name*)
for whom you gave Your Life.
Grant us priests
so that we may be fed from
the table of the Eucharist – the source
and summit of our lives.
Amen.

Fr Ruairi O'Domhnaill. Kildare & Leighlin

PRAYER FOR PRIESTS

Lord, grant your priests the goodness, strength and enthusiasm to follow you in all things;
to love the unloved, to nourish your people eucharistically and through your Word, to heal all who are ill in mind, body and spirit, to read the signs of the times and speak to people's hearts today, to bring the joy of the Gospel to where people are at in their lives, to listen to people, gently call to repentance and grant, with exuberant generosity, the forgiveness of sin, to speak your words of compassion even if rejected and never to despair of your plan of salvation for all people.

Guide and protect your priests, Lord, in times of loneliness, frustration and overwork, in times of temptation and weakness and when they feel they may have no more to offer. Strengthen them in their prayer life and to take time for reflection and refreshment in body and spirit. May they reflect your presence in the world and at the end of their days on Earth may you, dear Jesus, embrace them in the Father's House.
Amen.

Fr Richard Gibbons

HEALING
PRAYERS

RECONCILIATION / CONFESSIONS

One of the most important areas in Knock is the Chapel of Reconciliation or the Confessional – it is our engine room! People come simply to bring worries and sins before the Lord which weigh them down and ask for forgiveness which is always on offer!

There is no judgement, just mercy.

WHAT DO I DO?

1. Come before the Lord in quiet prayer.
2. Examine your conscience, in the light of the Ten Commandments and life of the Church.
3. Go to Confession.
4. Receive penance from the priest.
5. Say Act of Sorrow / Contrition.
6. Receive absolution.

BRIEF EXAMINATION OF CONSCIENCE

Have I called on God's name in vain?

Have I prayed?

Do I participate in Mass on Sundays and Holy
days?

Do I treat others honestly?

Do I spread lies, innuendos and rumours?

Do I respect family, parents, friends and strangers?

Do I respect my own body and the bodies of
others?

Do I respect God's gift of sexuality?

Do I steal or take from others?

Have I caused harm or violence to others?

Do I seek revenge for hurts caused?

Do I forgive?

Am I faithful to marriage vows?

Do I quarrel at home?

PRAYER BEFORE CONFESSION

....

God of all mercy, through your Son Jesus, you called
sinners to repent and believe in the Good News.
Help me to understand how I have not lived up to
my baptismal calling, personally and socially.
Guide me in making a good confession and
strengthen me in commitment to live my faith
joyfully.
Amen.

....

Fr Richard Gibbons

ACT OF CONTRITION

....

O my God I am sorry for all my sins,
for not loving others and not loving you,
help me to live like Jesus
and not sin again.
Amen.
O my God because you are so good,
I am very sorry that I have sinned
against you and by the help of your grace,
I will not sin again.
Amen.

SERENITY PRAYER

God grant me the serenity
to accept the things I cannot change;
courage to change the things I can;
and the wisdom to know the difference.
Living one day at a time,
Enjoying one moment at a time.
Accepting hardship as a pathway to peace,
taking as Jesus did, this sinful world as it is,
not as I would have it.
Trusting that you will make all things right
if I surrender to your will so that I may be
reasonably happy in this life and
supremely happy with you forever in the next.
Amen.

Reinhold Niebuhr

THE MIRACLE PRAYER

Lord Jesus, I come before you, just as I am.
I am sorry for my sins, I repent of my sins.
Please forgive me.
In your name, I forgive all others
for what they have done against me.
I renounce Satan,
The evil spirits and all their works.
I give you my entire self Lord Jesus,
now and forever.
I invite you into my life Lord Jesus.
I accept you as my Lord, God and Saviour.
Heal me, change me,
Strengthen me in body, soul and spirit.
Come Lord Jesus,
cover me with your precious blood
and fill me with your Holy Spirit.
I love you Lord Jesus,
I praise you Jesus, I thank you Jesus,
I shall follow you every day of my life.
Mary my Mother, Queen of Peace,
All the angels and saints, please help me.
Amen.

O SACRED HEART OF JESUS

O Sacred Heart of Jesus, I place all my trust in thee.
Whatever may befall me Lord,
tho' dark the hour may be,
In all my joys and all my woes
tho' nought but grief I see,
O Sacred Heart of Jesus, I place all my trust in thee.

When those I love have passed away
and I am sore distressed,
O Sacred Heart of Jesus,
I fly to thee for rest.
In all my trials great or small,
my confidence shall be
Unshaken, as I cry dear Lord,
I place my trust in thee.

This is my one great prayer dear Lord.
My faith my strong defence,
and most of all, in that last hour when
Death shall call me hence,
then dear Jesus may thy face
Smile on my soul set free,
O may I cry with rapturous joy,
I've placed all my trust in thee.
Amen.

NOVENA TO THE SACRED HEART

O Divine Jesus, who said, "Ask and you shall receive", I kneel at your feet. From whom shall I ask if not from you, whose heart is the source of all blessings. With a lively faith in you, I come to ask (mention request here) I admit I am most unworthy of your favours, O Jesus, but this is not a reason for me to be discouraged. You are the God of mercies and you will not refuse a contrite heart. Look with pity on me, I beg you, and your compassionate heart will find in my weakness a motive for granting my request.

Most Sacred Heart of Jesus, have mercy on us.

Amen.

OLD IRISH BLESSING

This day, and always,
May God's strength direct you,
May His power sustain you,
May His wisdom guide you,
And His vision light you.
His ear to your hearing,
His word to your speaking,
His hand to uphold you,
His pathway before you,
His shield to protect you,
And his legions to save you.
Amen.

A PRAYER IN TIME OF ILLNESS

....

Our Lady of Knock, in the depths of my illness and pain hear my voice as I ask you to intercede with your Son to heal me.

Walk with me Mary as I battle with pain, patience, frustration and helplessness.

Strengthen me in my time of need and help me to understand my illness. Bless all who care for me and may I once more know and enjoy the fullness of health.

Our Lady of Knock, pray for me.

Amen.

....

Fr Richard Gibbons

I LIGHT A CANDLE

I light a candle
And suddenly
the world about me
changes.
I am reminded
yet again
that one small flame
is all it takes
to let the darkness know
it cannot win.
Amen.

Dr Ruth Patterson. 'I Light A Candle'.

GRIEF

Grief cannot be shared, for it is mine alone.
Grief is a dying within me,
a great emptiness, a frightening void.
It is loneliness, a sickening sorrow at night,
on awakening a terrible dread.
Another's words do not help.
A reasoned argument explains little
for having tried too much.
Silence is the best response to another's grief.
Not the silence that is a pause in speech,
awkward and unwanted,
but one that unites heart to heart.
Love, speaking in silence, is the way into
the void of another's grief.
The best of all loves come silently,
and slowly too, to soften the pain of grief,
and begin to dispel the sadness.
It is the love of God, warm and true,
which will touch the grieving person and has pity,
and much else too, this Man of Sorrows.
He knows. He understands.
Grief will yield to peace – in time.
Amen.

Basil Cardinal Hume

Saints' Prayers

THE LORICA, OR BREASTPLATE
OF ST PATRICK

Christ with me, Christ before me,
Christ behind me, Christ within me,
Christ under me, Christ above me,
Christ at my right, Christ at my left.
Christ in lying down, Christ in sitting,
Christ in rising up.

Christ in the heart of everyone who thinks of me,
Christ in the mouth of everyone who speaks of me,
Christ in every eye that sees me,
Christ in every ear that hears me.

I bind to myself today
The strong power of an invocation of the Trinity,
The faith of the Trinity in Unity,
The Creator of the Universe.

Salvation is of the Lord,
Salvation is of the Lord,
Salvation is of Christ;
May Your salvation, O Lord, be with us forever.
Amen.

THE CANTICLE OF CREATION

....

Most high, all powerful, all good, Lord!
All praise is yours, all glory, all honour and all blessing.

To you alone, Most High, do they belong.
No mortal lips are worthy to pronounce your name.
All praise be yours, my Lord, with all that you have made, and first, my Lord, brother Sun, who brings the day, and light you give to us through him.
How beautiful is he, how radiant in all his splendour!
Of you, Most High, he bears the likeness.

All praise be yours, my Lord, through sister Moon and Stars;
in the heavens you have made them, bright and precious and fair.

All praise be yours, my Lord, through brothers Wind and Air,
and fair and stormy, all the weather's moods
by which you cherish all that you have made.

All praise be yours, my Lord, through sister Water,
so useful, so lowly, precious and pure.

All praise be yours, my Lord, through brother Fire,
through whom you brighten up the night.
How beautiful is he, full of power and strength!

All praise be yours, my Lord, through sister Earth,
our mother,
who feeds us in her sovereignty
and produces various fruits with coloured flowers
and herbs.

All praise be yours, my Lord,
through those who grant pardon for love of you;
through those who endure sickness and trial;
happy those who endure in peace;
by you, Most High, they will be crowned.

All praise be yours, my Lord, through sister Death,
from whose embrace no mortal can escape.
Woe to those who die in mortal sin;
happy those she finds doing your will.
The second death can do no harm to them.
Praise and bless my Lord,
and give him thanks and serve him with great
humility.
Amen.

St Francis of Assisi

PRAYER FOR PEACE

Lord, make me an instrument of your peace.
Where there is hatred, let me sow love,
where there is injury, pardon,
where there is doubt, faith
where there is despair, hope
where there is darkness, light
where there is sadness, joy
O Divine Master, grant that I may
not so much seek
to be consoled as to console;
to be understood as to understand;
to be loved as to love.
For it is in giving that we receive
it is in pardoning that we are pardoned
and it is in dying that we are born to eternal life.
Amen.

St Francis of Assisi

PRAYERS TO SAINTS

ST PATRICK

Saintly preacher, gentle priest,
Fearless man of God,
Give us, we pray, the strength to walk
The pathways you have trod.
Give us the strength to do the right
In spite of sword or spear,
The courage that makes heroes
Who know not craven fear.
You braved the might of princes,
You knew that they would yield,
God's grace your only weapon,
God's love your only shield.
Teach us your tact and gentleness,
Your love for Truth and Right,
Teach us to rule as you once ruled,
With kindly word, not might.
Teach us your art of preaching
By example more than word,
Teach us your own unselfishness
In the service of the Lord.
Amen.

Rev. T. Foy

ST BRIGID

You were a woman of peace.
You brought harmony where there was conflict.
You brought light to the darkness.
You brought hope to the downcast.
May the mantle of your peace
cover those who are troubled and anxious
and may peace be firmly rooted
in our hearts and in our world.
Inspire us to act justly
and to reverence all God has made.
Brigid, you were a voice
for the wounded and the weary.
Strengthen what is weak within us,
calm us into a quietness that heals and listens.
May we grow each day into greater wholeness in
    mind, body and spirit.
Amen.

ST ANTHONY – LOST OBJECTS

O Blessed St Anthony
the grace of God has made you
a powerful advocate in all our needs
and the person for the restoring
of things lost or stolen.
I turn to you today with love and confidence.
You have helped countless people to find
the things they have lost,
material things, and, more importantly
the things of the Spirit: faith, hope and love.
I come to you with confidence;
help me in my present need.
I recommend what I have lost to your care
in the hope that God will return it to me,
if it is His holy will.
Amen.

ST MICHAEL THE ARCHANGEL

St Michael the Archangel,
defend us in battle.
Be our safeguard against the wickedness and
snares of the Devil.
May God restrain him, we humbly pray,
and do thou,
O Prince of the heavenly hosts,
by the power of God,
thrust into hell Satan,
and with him all the wicked spirits,
who wander through the world
for the ruin of souls.
Amen.

Pope Leo XIII

ST JOSEPH

Blessed Joseph, husband of Mary,
be with us this day.
You protected and cherished the Virgin;
Loving the Child Jesus as your son,
You rescued him from danger of death.
Defend the Church, the household of God,
Purchased by the blood of Christ.
Guardian of the Holy Family,
Be with us in our trials.
May your prayers obtain for us
The strength to flee from error
And wrestle with the powers of corruption
So that in life we may grow in holiness
And in death rejoice in the crown of victory.
Amen.

ST ANNE

....

St Anne, mother of Mary, grandmother of Jesus, protect and guide all relationships with your care, especially family relationships which may be strained, difficult or broken.

Help us to be gentle, charitable and kind at all times. May your Grandson open us to His healing presence and grant us happiness in this life and the next. Amen.

....
Fr Richard Gibbons

ST JOHN THE BAPTIST

St John, as a prophet you prepared the way for the Son of God. As the baptiser you helped people acknowledge their sins, repent and reach a new understanding of God's presence in their lives. As martyr you gave witness to truth and justice in the world around you.

Help us to speak the truth of our faith today and not to be silenced or afraid, make us fully aware of our baptismal call to serve the Lord in the life of the Church.

Amen.

Fr Richard Gibbons

ST JOHN THE EVANGELIST

St John, beloved of the Lord, teacher of the Word of God and adopted son of Mary our Mother, deepen our faith in understanding the Word of God in our lives. Guide those who teach and preach the Word that they may do so in fidelity to the Church and at the same time making it relevant and meaningful in living our lives.

As you stood by the cross with Mary, your adopted mother, help us to bear our own crosses and never to lose sight of the Lord walking with us as we journey on our pilgrim path. May we understand that we are all adopted sons and daughters of God. Amen.

Fr Richard Gibbons

PRAYERS FOR CREATION

A CHRISTIAN PRAYER IN UNION WITH CREATION

. . . .

Father, we praise you with all your creatures.
They came forth from your all-powerful hand;
they are yours, filled with your presence and
your tender love.

Praise be to you!
Son of God, Jesus,
through you all things were made.
You were formed in the womb with human eyes.
Today you are alive in every creature
in your risen glory.

Praise be to you!
Holy Spirit, by your light
you guide this world towards the Father's love
and accompany creation as it groans in travail.
You also dwell in our hearts
and you inspire us to do what is good.

Praise be to you!
Triune Lord,
wondrous community of infinite love,
teach us to contemplate you
in the beauty of the universe,
for all things speak of you.

Awaken our praise and thankfulness
for every being that you have made.
Give us the grace to feel profoundly joined
to everything that is.

God of love, show us our place in this world
as channels of your love
for all the creatures of this earth,
for not one of them is forgotten in your sight.

Enlighten those who possess power and money
That they may avoid the sin of indifference,
that they may love the common good,
advance the weak,
and care for this world in which we live.

The poor and the Earth are crying out.
O Lord, seize us with your power and light,
help us to protect all life,
to prepare for a better future,
for the coming of your Kingdom
of justice, peace, love and beauty.
Praise be to you!
Amen.

Pope Francis, *Laudato Si*

TÍRECHÁN'S CREED

Our God is the God of all humans.
The God of Heaven and Earth.
The God of the sea and the rivers.
The God of the sun and moon.
The God of all the heavenly bodies.
The God of the lofty mountains.
The God of the lowly valleys.

God is above the heavens;
and he is in the heavens;
and he is beneath the heavens.
Heaven and Earth and sea,
and everything that is in them,
such he has as his abode.

He inspires all things,
he gives life to all things,
he stands above all things,
and he stands beneath all things.
He enlightens the light of the sun,
he strengthens the light of the night and the stars,
he makes wells in the arid land
and dry islands in the sea,
and he places the stars in the service
of the greater lights.

He has a Son who is co-eternal with himself,
and similar in all respects to himself;
and neither is the Son younger than the Father,
nor is the Father older than the Son;
and the Holy Spirit breathes in them.
And the Father and the Son and the Holy Spirit
are inseparable.
Amen.

Bishop Tírechán, 7th Century

FOR ALL ANIMALS

Blessed are you, Lord God,
maker of all living creatures.
On the fifth and sixth days of Creation,
you called forth fish in the sea,
birds in the air, and animals on the land.
You inspired St Francis to call all animals
his brothers and sisters.
We ask you to bless our animals.
By the power of your love,
Enable them to live according to your plan.
May we be faithful stewards and always praise you
for all your beauty in Creation.
Blessed are you, Lord our God, in all your creatures!
Amen.

Franciscan Animal Blessing

A LITTLE DOG'S PRAYER

A master who is firm and kind,
And understands a Doggie mind.
A "Walkie" and a meal each day,
is all I ask for when I pray.